MW00876853

A House for Wanda Wood Duck

Book Design by Cecile Birchler

Published by Ducks Unlimited, Inc.
L. J. Mayeux, President
Julius Wall, Chairman of the Board
D. A. (Don) Young, Executive Vice President

ISBN: 0-9617279-5-0
Published October 2001

Ducks Unlimited, Inc.
The mission of Ducks Unlimited is to fulfill the annual life cycle needs of North American waterfowl by protecting, enhancing, restoring, and managing important wetlands and associated uplands. Since its founding in 1937, DU has raised more than $1.3 billion, which has contributed to the conservation of over 9.4 million acres of prime wildlife habitat in all fifty states, each of the Canadian provinces, and in key areas of Mexico. In the U.S. alone, DU has helped to conserve over 2 million acres of waterfowl habitat. Some 900 species of wildlife live and flourish on DU projects, including many threatened and endangered species.

Printed in Canada

A House for Wanda Wood Duck

Patricia Barnes-Svarney

Illustrated by
Dominic Catalano

DUCKS UNLIMITED

It rained and rained that cold March.
It rained so hard the trees drooped.
It rained so long the frogs came out.
It rained so much, big puddles covered the ground.

Sarah and Jason looked out the kitchen window.
They missed their favorite wood duck,
a hen they named Wanda.

Every year, Wanda would come to the pond with her mate.
The ducks would swim and look for food together.
Then they would nest.
And every year, Wanda had several ducklings.

But not this year.
Wanda's favorite nesting site—a hole in a hollow tree—
had fallen down in one of the storms.
Wanda was nowhere in sight.

Sarah and Jason's father put his arms around their shoulders.
"Meet me in the garage," their father said.
"Maybe we can do something to help bring Wanda
back to the pond.
We can build a wood duck box for Wanda."

Sarah and Jason raced to the garage.

They watched as their father carved an egg-shaped hole in a piece of wood.

"This is so Wanda and her ducklings can get in and out of the wood box," he said.

Below the hole, Sarah and Jason helped their father hammer pieces of wire mesh.

"This is so Wanda and the ducklings can climb out of the box," he said.

They hammered the pieces of wood into a long box.

Jason easily lifted the top of the box.
"This is so we can get in and clean the box," he said.
Carefully, Sarah put chips of wood and sawdust
at the bottom of the box.
"This is so the ducklings and Wanda
have a soft place to sit," she said.
"And this," said their mother,
holding up a sign, "is for Wanda."
The sign read: "Wanda's House."

The next day, Sarah, Jason, and their parents walked to the edge of the pond.

Sarah and Jason carried the wood duck box.

Their parents carried a ladder.

"Here's a good spot," their father said. "We can see the box from our kitchen window."

He put the ladder against an old oak tree surrounded by water.

He lifted the box high off the ground and nailed it to the tree.

"Wanda's House should hold Wanda and her ducklings," he said.

The next day, Sarah and Jason watched out the kitchen window.
Something was moving in the tall reeds near the wood duck box.
"It's Wanda! She's back!" Sarah yelled, pointing to the pond.
"There's her mate!" Jason said, pointing to a drake near Wanda.
"And they see the wood duck box!" they cried together.

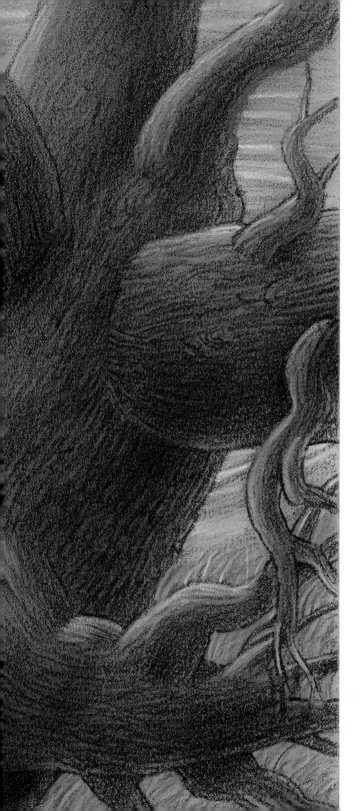

As Sarah and Jason watched, Wanda and her mate
swam around the base of the oak tree.
Wanda stretched her neck toward the box.
Then she flew into the box. It was time to lay her eggs.
"She likes it," Sarah whispered to Jason. Her brother nodded.

Every day, when Sarah and Jason came home from school,
they would run to the kitchen window.
"Did you see anything?" they would ask their parents.
"Just one of Wanda's hen friends," said their mother.
"It's too early for the eggs to hatch," said their father.

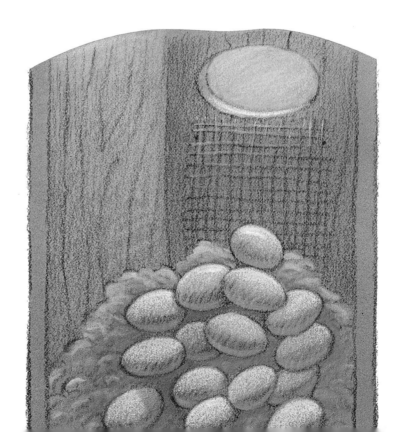

WANDA'S HOUSE

One night, the dog next door barked and barked.

Sarah and Jason raced to the kitchen window and shined a flashlight toward the wood duck box.

"Dad! Mom! A raccoon is trying to get into Wanda's House!" Sarah yelled.

Jason raised the window and yelled at the raccoon.

Their father yelled, too, and their mother beat a spoon on a frying pan.

"Shoo!" she cried.

The raccoon jumped from the box to the shore, then ran into the woods.

"I hope he didn't get any eggs," Sarah said.

"Me, too," said Jason.

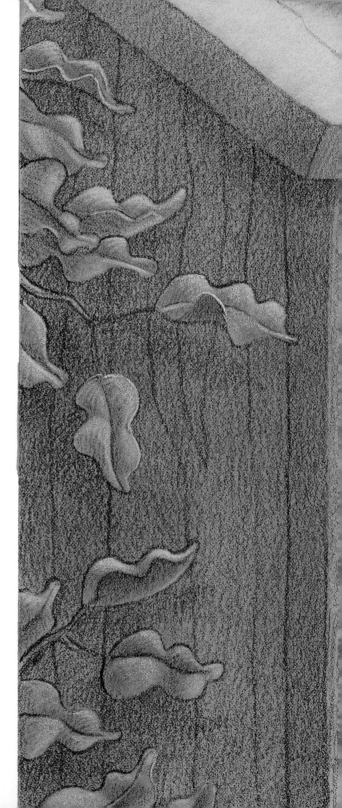

One long month later, sunshine warmed the ground.
Tiny buds were starting on the trees.
The tips of spring flowers burst from the ground.
It was much warmer than a month ago.

Sarah and Jason stood at the kitchen window.
They saw something moving below the "Wanda's House" sign.
A small head with a flat beak appeared at the hole.
Then it would pop back inside.

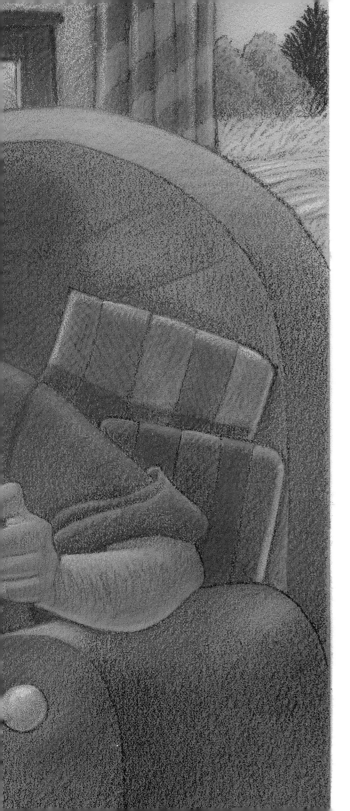

The ducklings were getting ready to leave the nest.
"Mom! Dad! They made it!
The raccoon didn't get the ducklings!"
Sarah and Jason yelled.

Wanda swam below the box.
It was time for the ducklings to swim.
Wanda made several clucking noises.
The first chick wiggled to the hole.

Out tumbled the first duckling—right into the water!
"Let's name him Woody," said Sarah, clapping her hands.
The second duckling fell into the water.
"Let's name her Wendy," said Jason.

Another duckling looked below at the water.
It looked too scared to jump.
It stood at the hole, stamped its tiny feet
and PLOP! fell right into the water.
"We'll name him Wilber!" Sarah and Jason said.

But the ducklings did not stop there.

Next came Wings, Walter, Wet Duck, Wide Duck, Wilma, and Wendell.

Then came Winnie, Weak Knees, and Willy.

And they kept coming.

"How many ducklings are there?" asked Sarah.

"We're running out of names!"

Suddenly, no ducklings were coming out of the box.

They were all in the water now, following Wanda in single file.

One...two...three...four...

"We counted 15 ducklings!" Sarah yelled to her parents.

"How many do wood ducks usually have?" asked Jason.

"Not *that* many," their father said. "It looks like Wanda's hen friend laid her eggs in the box, too."

"Wanda is going to have many ducklings to look after," their mother said.

For the next two months, Sarah and Jason
watched Wanda teach the ducklings
how to fly and look for food.
They watched as the ducklings grew and grew.
And they knew that next year Wanda
would come back to the pond and her special nest box.

Yes, next year they would see a whole new brood
of ducklings at "Wanda's House."

How to Build a Wood Duck Box

- Get a piece of weather-resistant lumber—1 inch thick, 12 inches wide, and 12 feet long.
- Measure and cut the board into separate pieces, as shown.
- Cut an oval hole—3 inches high and four inches wide—in the front panel.
- Tack a 1/4-inch piece of mesh hardware cloth to the inside of the front panel, as shown.
- Nail all the pieces together, except the roof.
- Attach the roof with hook-and-eye fasteners, as shown.

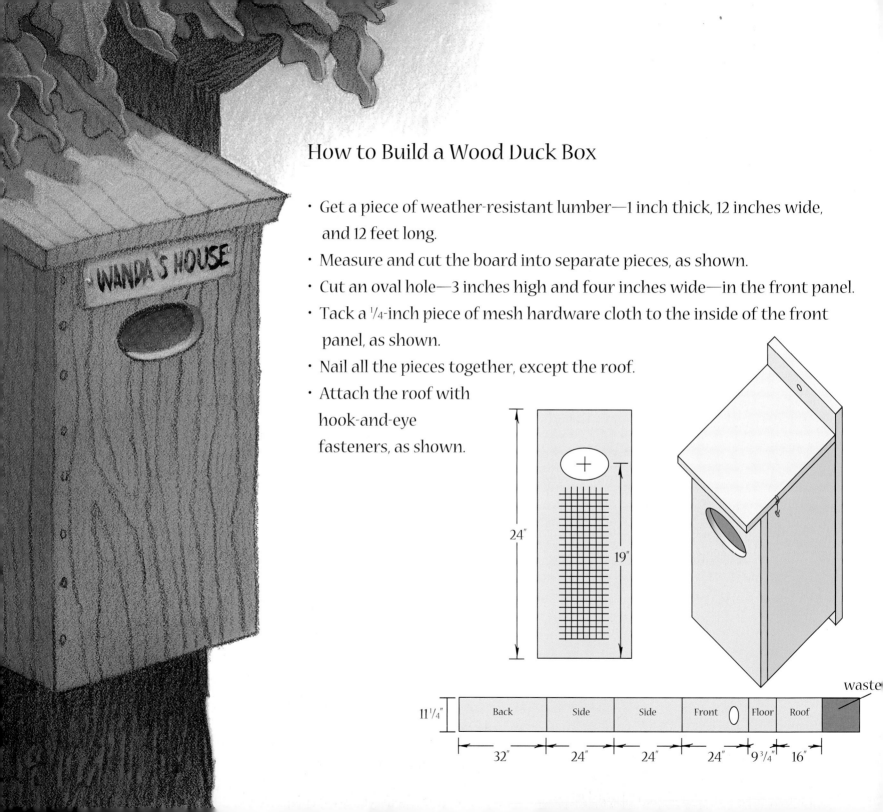

24"

19"

waste

Back	Side	Side	Front O	Floor	Roof	

11 1/4"

32"   24"   24"   24"   9 3/4"   16"